SPECIAL
DAYS
AUSTRALIA
DAY
JANE PFEIFFER
REDBACK
publishing

First published 2023 by
Redback Publishing
PO Box 357 Frenchs Forest NSW 2086
Australia

www.redbackpublishing.com
orders@redbackpublishing.com

ISBN 978-1-76140-023-0 PBK

Author: Jane Pfeiffer
Editor: Caroline Thomas
Design: Redback Publishing

Original illustrations © Redback Publishing 2023
Originated by Redback Publishing

Printed and bound in Malaysia

Acknowledgements
Abbreviations: l—left, r—right, b—bottom, t—top, c—centre, m—middle
We would like to thank the following for permission to reproduce photographs: (Images © shutterstock, wikimediacommons)
pg6-7 superjoseph / Shutterstock.com, pg8m Aldo Manganaro / Shutterstock.com, pg9t Holli / Shutterstock.com, pg11b sduraku / Shutterstock.com, pg12bl Collywolly, CC BY-SA 4.0 (https://creativecommons.org/licenses/by-sa/4.0), via Wikimedia Commons, pg14mr Department of Foreign Affairs and Trade website – www.dfat.gov.au, CC BY 3.0 AU (https://creativecommons.org/licenses/by/3.0/au/deed.en), via Wikimedia Commons, pg14bl Marco Taliani de Marchio / Shutterstock.com, pg15tl Jaeplayboy / Shutterstock.com, pg17br Tralis2, CC BY-SA 4.0 (https://creativecommons.org/licenses/by-sa/4.0), via Wikimedia Commons, pg18-19 Dave Snowden, CC BY-SA 2.0 (https://creativecommons.org/licenses/by-sa/2.0), via Wikimedia Commons, pg21mr DIAC images, CC BY 2.0 (https://creativecommons.org/licenses/by/2.0), via Wikimedia Commons, pg27br Bidgee, CC BY-SA 3.0 AU (https://creativecommons.org/licenses/by-sa/3.0/au/deed.en), via Wikimedia Commons, pg26m Olga Kashubin / Shutterstock.com,

A catalogue record for this book is available from the National Library of Australia

CONTENTS

SPECIAL DAYS

In Australia we celebrate or commemorate a number of special days throughout the year. Some are public holidays, which means people can have the day off work or school. Some special days are marked with events and festivities.

Many special days in Australia commemorate something of historical importance. This gives Australians the opportunity to recognise how people and events have shaped our nation. Australia is a multicultural society with a Federation of states and territories. Some special days are significant only to a particular state. Some are important to a specific culture, community or religious group.

Special days are a chance to reflect on the past, to appreciate the world we know, and to look to the future together. On these days, we celebrate some of the things that make Australia what it is today.

Australia is a federation of states and territories, so some special days are significant only to a particular state.

AUSTRALIA DAY

All states and territories mark Australia Day on 26 January each year. It is a public holiday that allows people to reflect on what it means to be Australian. The date marks the 1788 arrival of the First Fleet from Britain, which began the European colonisation of Australia. It is a time to reflect on the ongoing impact of European arrival on Aboriginal people, for whom it is both a day of mourning and a time to celebrate their survival and endurance.

It is also a day to celebrate Australia's rich migrant history that began with convict transportation. Today, approximately 200,000 people migrate to Australia each year. On Australia Day, people celebrate Australian values such as getting a 'fair go', democracy and freedom, and being thankful for a safe and prosperous land.

DAY: Australia Day
DATE: 26 January
WHERE: All states and territories
WHAT: A public holiday that marks the official national day of Australia

Different people mark Australia Day in different ways. Formal celebrations include Citizenship Ceremonies, the announcement of the Australia Day Honours, and flag-raising ceremonies. Some people attend Dawn Services to honour the Aboriginal peoples who died during the frontier wars. Cultural festivals and community events and celebrations are held around the nation. Many people choose to spend this special day enjoying time with their families and friends at the beach, bushwalking or simply appreciating the country they call home.

SURVIVAL DAY

For Aboriginal people, 26 January marks the end of a way of life and the beginning of their survival. The Aboriginal people had thrived on the land, now known as Australia, for over 60,000 years, but colonisation brought disease and violence that reduced the Aboriginal population by around 90 percent. Today, the number of Aboriginal people living in Australia has grown to about 800,000.

Australia Day is also when many Aboriginal people celebrate Survival Day. This reflects the endurance of the oldest continuing culture in the world, despite colonisation, discrimination and inequality. The voices of Aboriginal people are becoming more widely heard, and non-Indigenous people are beginning to value Aboriginal people's knowledge, opinion and traditions. Formal reconciliation began in 1991 and it continues today.

ULURU, A SACRED INDIGENOUS SITE

Survival Day has become a day of hope, with festivals, concerts, cultural events and ceremonies held in all states and territories around Australia. Events include live music and storytelling, traditional foods and arts stalls, craft workshops, smoking ceremonies and traditional dancing.

In Sydney, the Survival Day concert has been held annually since 1992. It is a family event where people come together to celebrate Indigenous culture. All states and territories also hold Invasion Day marches and rallies to raise awareness of ongoing land ownership and sovereignty matters.

THE IMPORTANCE OF DATES

Australia Day is intended as a celebration of what makes Australia great. This includes its British heritage, the evolution of its government including Federation, the contribution of migrants, and the modern day values and freedoms of the people who call Australia home.

Because 26 January represents invasion and loss for Aboriginal people, there is ongoing debate around whether or not Australia's national day should be moved to a different date. Aboriginal people have been protesting the date of Australia Day for over 80 years. On 26 January, 1938, the Australian Natives Association held the first official Day of Mourning.

Most people agree that Australia should celebrate its national day in a way that is inclusive of everyone, and that celebrates a future with a united population. Australia Day is as much about creating a sense of belonging as it is about commemorating the past. Many people believe that combining Australia Day with Survival Day encourages the celebration of all things Australian.

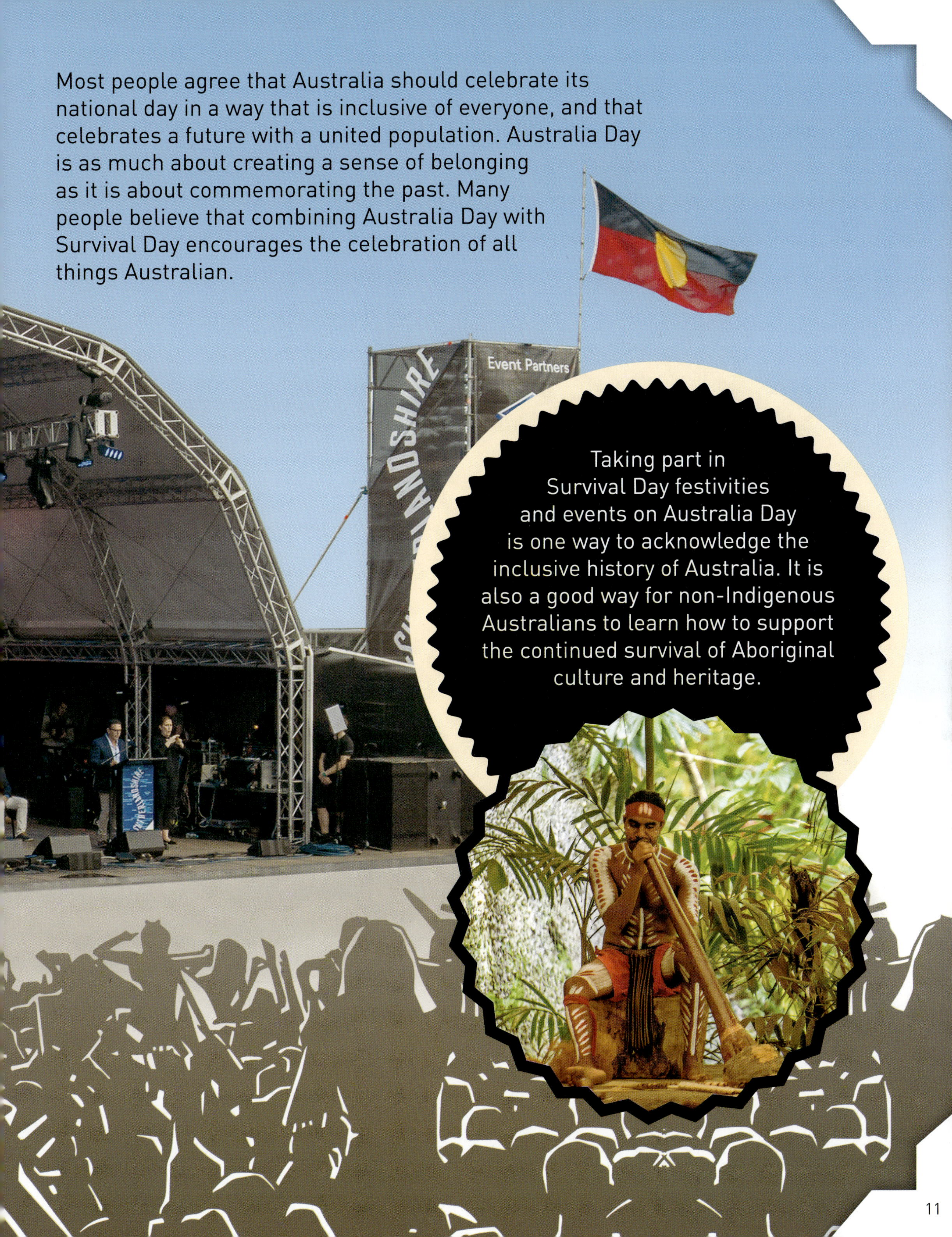

Taking part in Survival Day festivities and events on Australia Day is one way to acknowledge the inclusive history of Australia. It is also a good way for non-Indigenous Australians to learn how to support the continued survival of Aboriginal culture and heritage.

THE FIRST AUSTRALIA DAY

On 26 January, 1788, Captain Arthur Phillip landed at Sydney Cove, planted the British flag and ordered men to begin clearing ground for an encampment. The site was to become the first British convict settlement in the colony of New South Wales. This landing was the official arrival of the First Fleet of eleven ships carrying exiled prisoners from Britain. Twenty years later, records show that there were anniversary celebrations, but it took another ten years for the first official celebration to be held in 1818. Governor Macquarie named the day Foundation Day, and ordered a thirty-gun salute, followed by a special dinner and a ball at Dawes Point in Sydney.

To commemorate the First Fleet, a sailing regatta was held in Sydney in 1837. Now known as the Australia Day Regatta, this tradition has continued every year since.

In 1838, Foundation Day was declared a public holiday in New South Wales. It was the first Australian public holiday ever to be granted. Celebrations took place on the foreshore including community picnics and fireworks at the end of the day.

By 1935, New South Wales had begun to call the 26 January Australia Day, and by 1946 all other states and territories used that name too.

In 1994, Australia Day became a public holiday in all states and territories, so that all Australians could celebrate together.

THE CONVICT LEGACY

Modern Australia is a result of its proud multicultural history and the Australian population now includes migrants from over 190 countries. This history of immigration began with the First Fleet, and over 8,000 of their descendants still call Australia home. In the 80 years that followed the first arrival, over 164,000 convicts came to Australia.

Men, women and children were sentenced to transportation for a range a crimes. Since most serious crimes were punishable by death at that time, very few dangerous criminals came to Australia. The most common crime that resulted in the sentence of transportation was petty theft.

Some convicts played an important part in building the nation. Mary Wade was just 11 years old when she was sentenced to transportation for the crime of stealing another girl's clothes. Mary went on to help build the population of Australia by having 21 children.
At the time of her death, she had over 300 descendants and is considered one of the founding mothers of Australia. Her most famous descendant, Kevin Rudd, became the 26th Prime Minister of Australia.

KEVIN RUDD

Francis Greenway was convicted of forgery and sentenced to transportation. He later worked as a government architect designing several important buildings that still stand today. His work includes the First Government House in Sydney, the Sydney Conservatorium of Music, the Macquarie Lighthouse and St. James's Church in Sydney.

FRANCIS GREENWAY

SYDNEY CONSERVATORIUM OF MUSIC

AUSTRALIA DAY HONOURS

The Australia Day Honours system was established in 1975. These awards are to thank and acknowledge those who have given outstanding service to their community, or who have achieved something that has greatly benefitted their community. There are awards for many different areas of contribution, from military service to the arts. Honours are awarded for bravery, service to the community, or achievement in a particular occupation.

Anyone in the community can put an Australian citizen's name forward for the award. The Order of Australia Council chooses which names to recommend to the Governor General, who then approves the final list. In 2020, 1,099 people received an Australia Day Honour. Over 41 percent of those recipients were women, which is the highest percentage of women in the history of the awards. The honours were awarded to a diverse range of people who make extraordinary contributions to Australia. In 2020, these people included a plumber, a molecular biologist, a high school principal and a conservationist.

PARLIAMENT HOUSE, CANBERRA

AUSTRALIAN OF THE YEAR AWARD

The Australian of the Year Award recognises the outstanding work of public individuals. The choice of nominees also highlights Australia's changing national identity over time, as the recipients reflect the country's current needs and interests. The Australian of the Year Awards are a highlight of Australia Day celebrations, and the official announcement in Canberra forms part of a nationally televised ceremony.

THE AWARD CATEGORIES ARE:

- Australian of the Year
- Senior Australian of the Year
- Young Australian of the Year
- Local Hero

LOCAL HERO 2020

Founder of the BackTrack Youth Works Program in Armidale, Bernie Shakeshaft, has made an enormous difference to over 1,000 children, supporting them and giving them hope for their future

YOUNG AUSTRALIAN OF THE YEAR 2018

Sportsperson Samantha Kerr was recognised for her exceptional soccer career and as a role model for young women.

SENIOR AUSTRALIAN OF THE YEAR 2017

Sister Anne Gardiner AM was awarded Senior Australian of the Year in 2017 for her many decades of work supporting Tiwi culture and celebrating Aboriginal heritage.

AUSTRALIAN OF THE YEAR 2020

Dr James Muecke AM was recognised for his work as an eye surgeon and blindness prevention pioneer.

AUSTRALIANS OF THE YEAR 2019

Dr Richard Harris and Dr Craig Challen were joint recipients of the 2019 Australians of the Year Award for their heroic efforts rescuing twelve boys from flooded caves in Thailand.

CITIZENSHIP CEREMONIES

The high standard of living in Australia is known worldwide and, for the last seven years, the Global Liveability Index has named Melbourne the second best city to live in the world. Many people migrate to Australia each year, for many different reasons. Besides the beautiful landscapes, rich culture, and education and work opportunities, some migrants simply seek the right to basic things that Australians take for granted. Australians can expect peaceful living, safe drinking water, reliable food supply, democracy and law, as well as human rights and liberties.

MELBOURNE CBD

Becoming an Australian citizen not only means being allowed to live in Australia permanently, it allows a person to vote and serve in government, to serve in the military, and to serve on a jury to help uphold the laws which keep people safe. In 2019-2020, a total of 204,817 people became new Australian citizens, representing over 200 different nationalities. This was an increase of 60 percent from the previous year and the highest number ever recorded. One reason for this increase was a switch to online ceremonies amid the coronavirus pandemic.

On Australia Day, citizenship ceremonies are held all over Australia. New citizens take the Australian Citizenship Pledge, to accept both the privileges and the responsibilities of being an Australian citizen. Responsibilities include upholding Australian laws and respecting the rights and freedoms of others. There are two pledges to choose from, which are identical except for the mention of God.

PLEDGE 1

From this time forward, under God,
I pledge my loyalty to Australia and its people,
whose democratic beliefs I share,
whose rights and liberties I respect, and
whose laws I will uphold and obey.

PLEDGE 2

From this time forward,
I pledge my loyalty to Australia and its people,
whose democratic beliefs I share,
whose rights and liberties I respect, and
whose laws I will uphold and obey.

THE AMBASSADOR PROGRAM

Australia Day Ambassadors support Australia Day events and celebrations by inspiring national pride. They usually showcase diversity as well as achievement. Each year, over 300 high achieving Australians and past Australian of the Year recipients volunteer to be Australia Day Ambassadors. They attend local celebrations in cities, towns and regional areas all over the country to make speeches, present awards and help judge competitions. The Ambassador Program began in 1990, with just nine ambassadors.

Nineteen-year old Macinley Butson served as an Australia Day Ambassador in 2020. She had received the NSW Young Australian of the Year Award in 2018 for her exceptional contributions as a young inventor and scientist. Macinley spoke at the Australia Day event in Hay, New South Wales to inspire other young people in the field of science.

NSW 2019 Volunteer of the Year, Robert Fitzgerald, served as an Australia Day Ambassador in 2020. He was invited to an Australia Day breakfast in Forbes, New South Wales to talk to the community about the importance and benefits of volunteering.

RAISING THE FLAGS

Australia has three official flags: the Australian national flag, the Australian Aboriginal flag and the Torres Strait Islander flag. Each state and territory also has its own flag. Flag raising ceremonies are an important part of Australia Day events. As the country's foremost symbol, the Australian national flag should be used with respect and dignity. On Australia Day, the Australian flag is flown together with the Aboriginal flag and the Torres Strait Islander flag. The Australian national flag must not be smaller than either the Aboriginal or Torres Strait Islander flags, and they must be flown in that order from left to right. A state or territory flag must be placed after the national flag. Flags should never be flown upside down.

THE AUSTRALIAN NATIONAL FLAG

Australia's national flag was first flown on 3 September, 1901, at the Royal Exhibition Building in Melbourne.

- The Union Jack represents British settlement.
- The Southern Cross represents Australia's geographic position in the Southern Hemisphere.
- The Commonwealth star on the left represents Federation.

ROYAL EXHIBITION BUILDING IN MELBOURNE

THE AUSTRALIAN ABORIGINAL FLAG

Aboriginal artist, Harold Thomas, designed the Australian Aboriginal Flag for National Aborigines Day in July, 1971. In 1972, it became the official flag flown at the Aboriginal Tent Embassy in Canberra and was declared one of Australia's national flags in July, 1995.

- Black represents the Aboriginal people.
- The yellow circle represents the sun.
- Red (ochre) represents the earth.

THE TORRES STRAIT ISLANDER FLAG

In 1992, the Torres Strait Islander people held a cultural revival that included a flag design competition. Bernard Namok Snr's design won, and the new flag was flown at the Cultural Festival in May, 1992. It was recognised as an official flag of Australia on 14 July, 1995.

- Green represents the land.
- Blue represents the waters of the Torres Strait.
- Two black stripes represent the people.
- The central symbol is a white Dhari, which is a traditional headdress.
- The five-pointed white star symbolises peace between the five major island groups of the Torres Strait.

AUSTRALIA DAY AROUND AUSTRALIA

Australia Day events need to appeal to a diverse range of people within a community. All around Australia, large events need careful planning that involves lots of different people. Special committees help to make sure Aboriginal people, ethnic communities and other local community groups are all involved in deciding what the day will involve. Free events often include cultural exhibitions, workshops and demonstrations, as well as live entertainment. Australia Day parades, community picnics, boat races, concerts and festivals usually follow any formal affairs. Festivities often continue into the night with fireworks in most capital cities.

CORROBOREE PERFORMANCE AT YABUN FESTIVAL, SYDNEY, 2020

BRISBANE, 2017

WELCOME TO COUNTRY

Australia Day events often begin with a Welcome To Country. The official Welcome of visitors is an Aboriginal and Torres Strait Islander tradition that dates back thousands of years. An Aboriginal or Torres Strait Islander who is a traditional owner, custodian, or Elder of the local area conducts this special ceremony to welcome people to their land. The ceremony may be a combination of a speech, song and traditional music, and ceremonial dance. An Acknowledgement of Country usually follows the Welcome to Country. A non-Indigenous person can give the Acknowledgement of Country, which recognises the traditional owners of the land on which they stand and pays respect to their Elders both past and present.

WIRADJURI ELDER, AUNTY ISOBEL REID, GIVING A WELCOME TO COUNTRY

AUSTRALIA DAY AROUND THE WORLD

There are no ceremonies overseas for new citizens or the Australia Day Awards, but celebrations that honour Australian culture and everyday life are very popular with Australians living far from home. Many Australians living overseas will eat Australian food, play Australian games, and listen to Australian music to remind themselves of home.

USA

Los Angeles, New York, Chicago and Washington are just some of the cities in the USA that hold large-scale events to celebrate Australian culture. G'Day USA holds cross-cultural events throughout the year and high profile Australian celebrities attend the G'Day USA Australia Day Black Tie Gala in Los Angeles.

UNITED KINGDOM

London has one of the largest populations of Australian expatriates in the world. On Australia Day, both formal and informal events are held across the city; cinemas show Australian movies, restaurants serve Australian food and bars feature live Australian music. Some theatres hold Australian comedy shows, while Australian celebrities attend formal Gala Dinners.

THAILAND

Australian Embassies around the world often hold official receptions to celebrate Australia Day. In Thailand, distinguished guests from other governments and embassies attend Australia Day receptions.

OUR NATIONAL DAY

Australia's national day represents a celebration of national pride. There is much that Australians can be very proud of and it is official; Australia is one of the best places to live in the whole world.

Some people would like Australia's national day to be free of sadness and mourning, so that they can freely celebrate the successes and joys of all things Australian, without upsetting Aboriginal people. While 26 January will always be an important day, there is ongoing debate as to whether or not it is the special date that should represent modern Australia. Some people choose to celebrate their Australian pride on a different date. Whichever date you choose to celebrate Australia, remember that its history is still being written. What would you like the next 200 years to look like?

GLOSSARY

citizenship recognition by government that a person is a member of a nation

colonisation process of gaining control over land and the people who were already living there

commemorate honour the memory of something with a ceremony or celebration

discrimination treating people unfairly due to difference

endurance ability to resist and withstand something unpleasant for a long time

evolution continued change and development of something over time

exiled period of forced absence from a person's native country

expatriate person who lives outside their native country

Federation bringing together of a group of colonies into one nation

gala big event and celebration

honour to show a great respect for a person or group of people

inequality unfair difference in the quality of life or treatment of a person

mourning expression of sadness in relation to someone's death

multicultural referring to different nationalities coming together and accepting each other's cultures

reconciliation process of finding a way forward so that two opposing parties can achieve mutual respect

sense of belonging feeling part of a group

thrived had good health and success

transportation punishment for convicted criminals that involved being sent to a distant place

INDEX